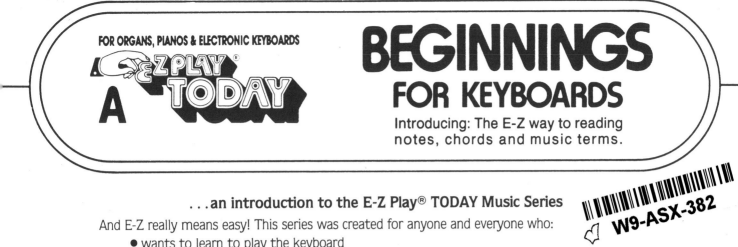

FOR ORGANS, PIANOS & ELECTRONIC KEYBOARDS

E-Z PLAY TODAY

A

BEGINNINGS
FOR KEYBOARDS
Introducing: The E-Z way to reading notes, chords and music terms.

W9-ASX-382

...an introduction to the E-Z Play® TODAY Music Series

And E-Z really means easy! This series was created for anyone and everyone who:

- wants to learn to play the keyboard
- doesn't have time to take music lessons
- wants to play popular songs and favorite tunes instantly!

Keyboard instruments are among the most versatile of all musical instruments. And many electronic keyboards today have special automatic features and automatic rhythms. All of the arrangements are versatile, too, because they can be played on:

- a chord organ
- an electronic keyboard with one-key chord accompaniment and automatic rhythm
- a conventional keyboard instrument without automatic features

In other words, E-Z Play TODAY Music is for **all keyboards** and for **all keyboard players.**

BEGINNINGS will show you how to play with a minimum of effort...and a maximum of pleasure. Just turn the page and BEGIN your musical adventure with BEGINNINGS!

NOTE: There is a supplementary songbook now available that works with EZ Play Today BEGIN-NINGS For Keyboards instruction books A, B and C. There is a cross-reference chart at the end of SUPPLEMENTARY SONGBOOK A, B, C that shows where the songs in that book fit with the songs in this book. In addition, at the beginning of each song in the sup-plementary songbook, there is a cross-reference to the instruction books.

Contents

HAL•LEONARD®
CORPORATION
7777 W. BLUEMOUND RD. P.O. BOX 13819 MILWAUKEE, WI 53213

This publication is not for sale in the E.C. and/or Australia or New Zealand.

NOTATION

All songs are written in the exclusive E-Z Play TODAY music notation.

- A STAFF is five lines with spaces between them. Each line or space represents a lettered note.

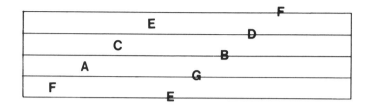

- Sometimes LEDGER LINES are added above or below the staff to accommodate additional notes.

LEDGER LINES ─────

─────── **LEDGER LINES**

- The lettered notes correspond to lettered keys on the keyboard guide. As notes move down the staff, the corresponding keys move down (to the left) on the keyboard. As the notes move up the staff, they move up (to the right) on the keyboard.

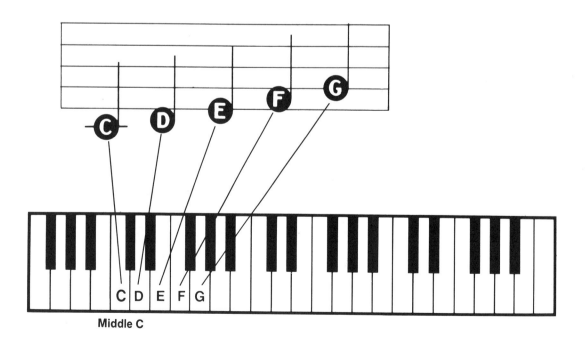

Middle C

NOTE VALUES

- Each type of note has a specific TIME VALUE which is measured in rhythmic beats.

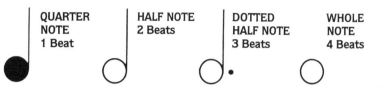

| QUARTER NOTE 1 Beat | HALF NOTE 2 Beats | DOTTED HALF NOTE 3 Beats | WHOLE NOTE 4 Beats |

- Each staff is divided by BAR LINES into sections called MEASURES. A DOUBLE BAR indicates the end of a song.

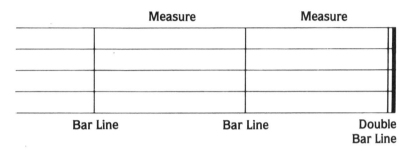

- A TIME SIGNATURE appears at the beginning of each song after the TREBLE CLEF sign.

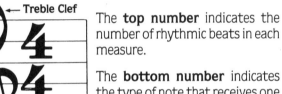

← Treble Clef

4 beats in each measure

A quarter note gets one beat

The **top number** indicates the number of rhythmic beats in each measure.

The **bottom number** indicates the type of note that receives one beat. 4 indicates a quarter note.

3 beats in each measure

A quarter note gets one beat

- Sometimes a note or notes appear at the beginning of a song that do not equal the number of beats indicated by the time signature. These are called PICKUP NOTES, and the missing beats are written at the end of the song.

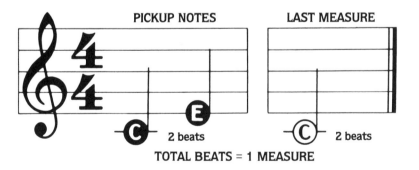

PICKUP NOTES

LAST MEASURE

C — 2 beats

E

C — 2 beats

TOTAL BEATS = 1 MEASURE

- A TIE is a curved line that connects notes of the same pitch (notes on the same line or space). Play the first note and then hold for the total time of all tied notes.

2 BEATS + 4 BEATS = 6 BEATS   **4 BEATS + 4 BEATS = 8 BEATS**

A CHORD SYSTEM FOR EVERYONE!

Chord accompaniment can be played in two ways. Read the following information carefully, then select the chord system you prefer.

1 ONE-BUTTON (Chord Organ) or ONE-KEY CHORDS — If you have a chord organ or a one-key chord unit on your instrument, press and hold the button or key indicated by the chord symbol. Each button or key produces a three- or four-note chord sound with a corresponding bass tone.

2 STANDARD CHORD POSITIONS — When playing standard chord positions, the positions (inversions) of the three- and four-note chords are strictly matters of your own choice. The suggested positions and fingerings for the C, G, and F chords are shown below. Bass pedals are often played with standard chord positions, although on some instruments the bass is produced automatically.

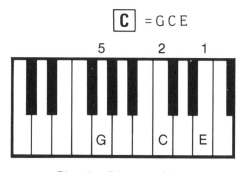

Play the C bass pedal.

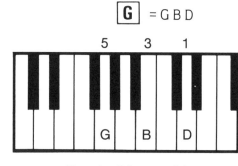

Play the G bass pedal.

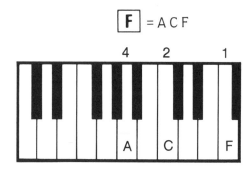

Play the F bass pedal.

For your reference, a CHORD SPELLER of commonly used standard chord positions is included at the back of this book.

When The Saints Go Marching In

Registration 2

Negro spiritual

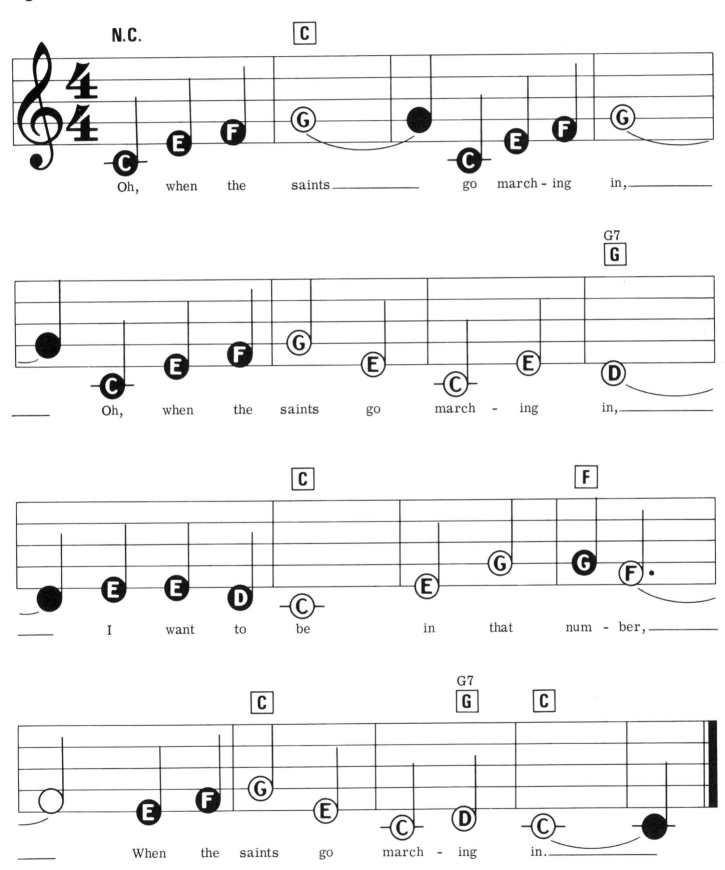

AUTOMATIC RHYTHM

The excitement created by an automatic rhythm will enhance your music regardless of which left-hand chord system you select. Here are a few hints for the most effective use of your rhythm unit:

- Experiment with the various rhythms available on your unit. Select a rhythm pattern that complements each song. Sometimes it's fun to create an unusual or different mood by selecting a rhythm pattern not generally associated with the song. For example, you might try a rock rhythm with WHEN THE SAINTS GO MARCHING IN.

- Most rhythm units have a volume control which regulates the volume level of the percussion instruments. For Latin rhythms, the percussion instruments usually play a more prominent role than they do in a ballad type rhythm; therefore adjust the volume control accordingly.

- Every rhythm unit has a tempo (speed) control which regulates the speed of the selected rhythm pattern. As you first begin to learn a song, adjust the tempo control to a slower speed until you can play the song with ease and accuracy.

- The tempo light flashes at predetermined time intervals. Watch the light for the speed of the rhythm and also to determine when a rhythm pattern begins.

Play WHEN THE SAINTS GO MARCHING IN again, this time adding an appropriate automatic rhythm, such as Swing, Ballad, Dixieland, or Rock.

INTRODUCING - NEW NOTES

In the next two songs, there are three new notes...A, B, and another C.

● They appear like this on the staff.

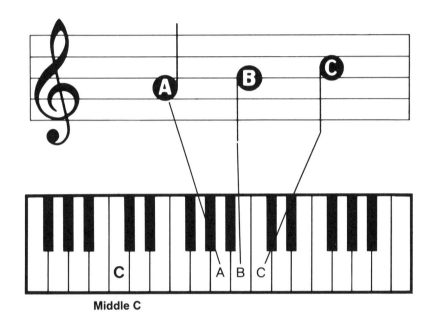

Middle C

● They correspond to these keys on the keyboard.

INTRODUCING - NEW NOTES

New D, E, and F notes are introduced in the next melodies.

● They appear like this on the staff.

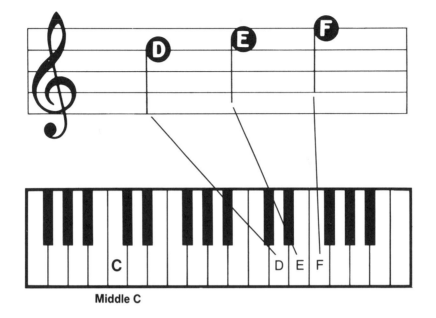

Middle C

● They correspond to these keys on the keyboard.

INTRODUCING - RESTS

Rests indicate periods of silence. They correspond to the time values of notes having the same name.

QUARTER REST	HALF REST	WHOLE REST
1 Beat	2 Beats	4 Beats

INTRODUCING - REPEAT SIGNS AND 1ST AND 2ND ENDINGS

Repeat Signs

Repeat Signs are used in a song when a section of the arrangement or the entire song is to be played again (repeated). Generally, Repeat Signs appear in sets of two.

- There will be one repeat sign (A) at the beginning of the section to be repeated.

- Play up to the repeat sign at the end of this section (B).

- Return to the first repeat sign (A) and play the section again.

- If there is no repeat sign (A), return to the beginning of the song.

1st and 2nd Endings

When two different endings appear within or at the end of a song, here's what to do:

- Play the song up through the first (1) ending.

- Repeat to the closest repeat sign, or back to the beginning.

- Play that section again, skip the first ending (1), but play the second ending (2).

Village Polka

Registration 5
Rhythm: Polka or March

Traditional

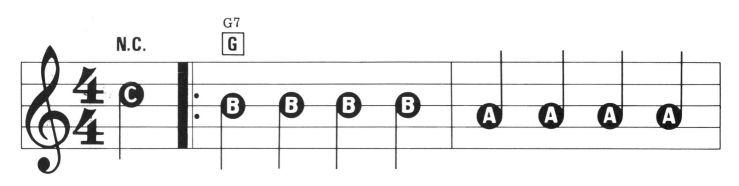

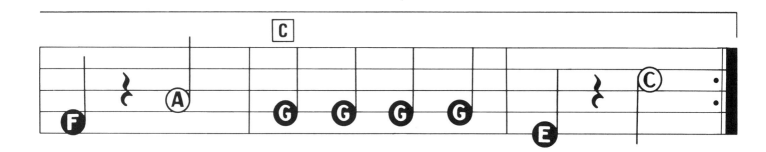

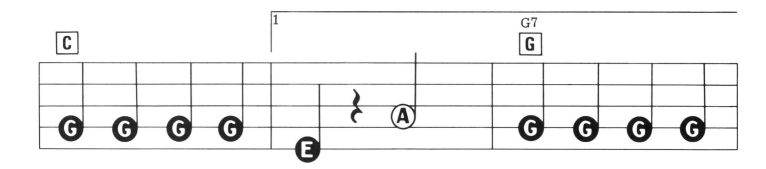

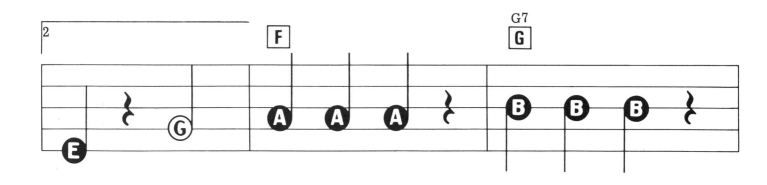

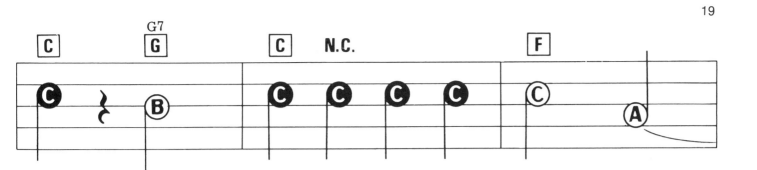

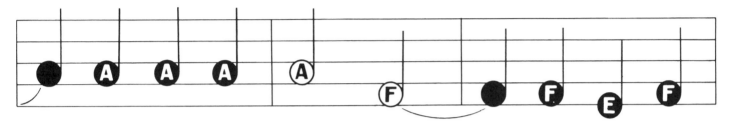

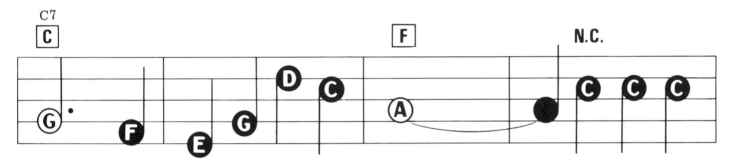

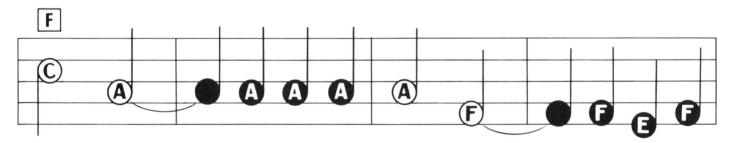

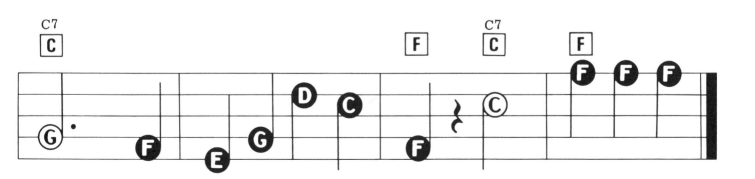

Beautiful Brown Eyes

Registration 1
Rhythm: Waltz

Traditional

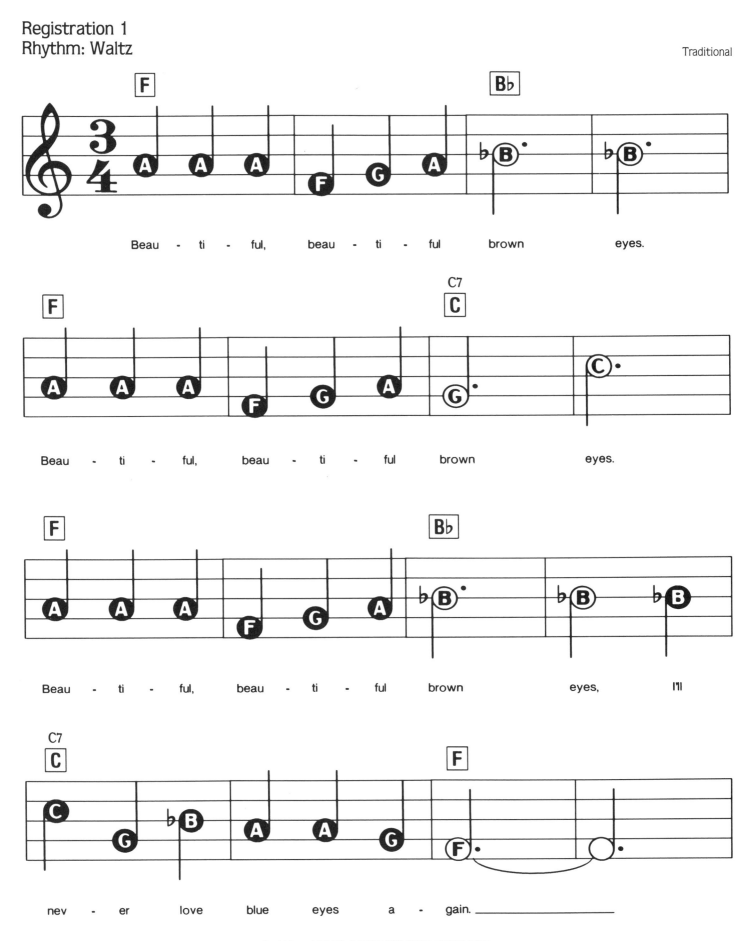

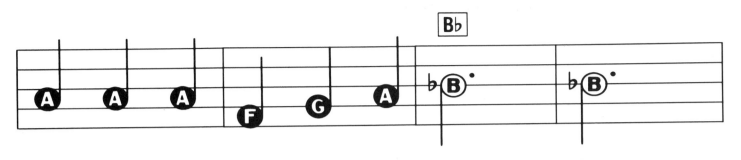

Beau - ti - ful, beau - ti - ful brown eyes.

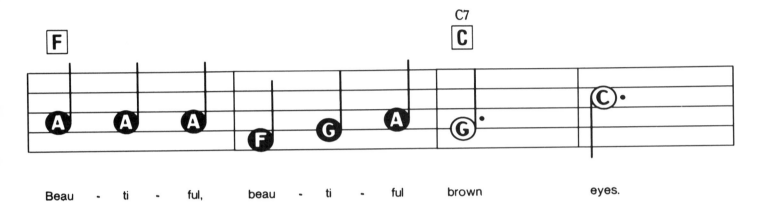

Beau - ti - ful, beau - ti - ful brown eyes.

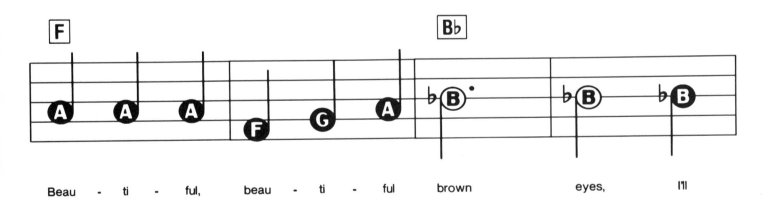

Beau - ti - ful, beau - ti - ful brown eyes, I'll

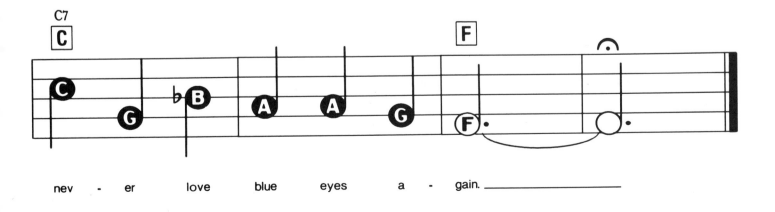

nev - er love blue eyes a - gain. _____

INTRODUCING - A NEW CHORD: Dm

- ONE KEY or CHORD BUTTON — Locate the key(s) or button labeled Dm. Consult your owner's manual for information on playing one-key minor chords.

- STANDARD CHORD — Dm = A D F

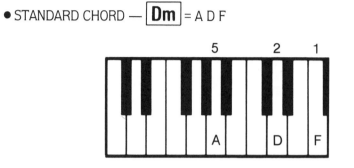

On Top Of Old Smoky

Registration 1
Rhythm: Waltz

Appalachian

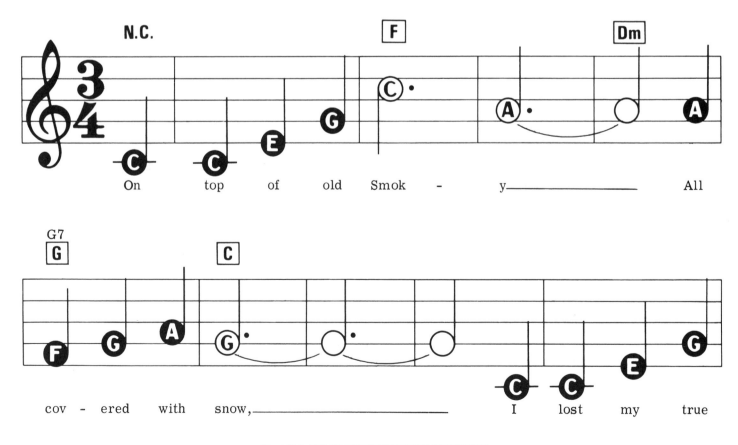

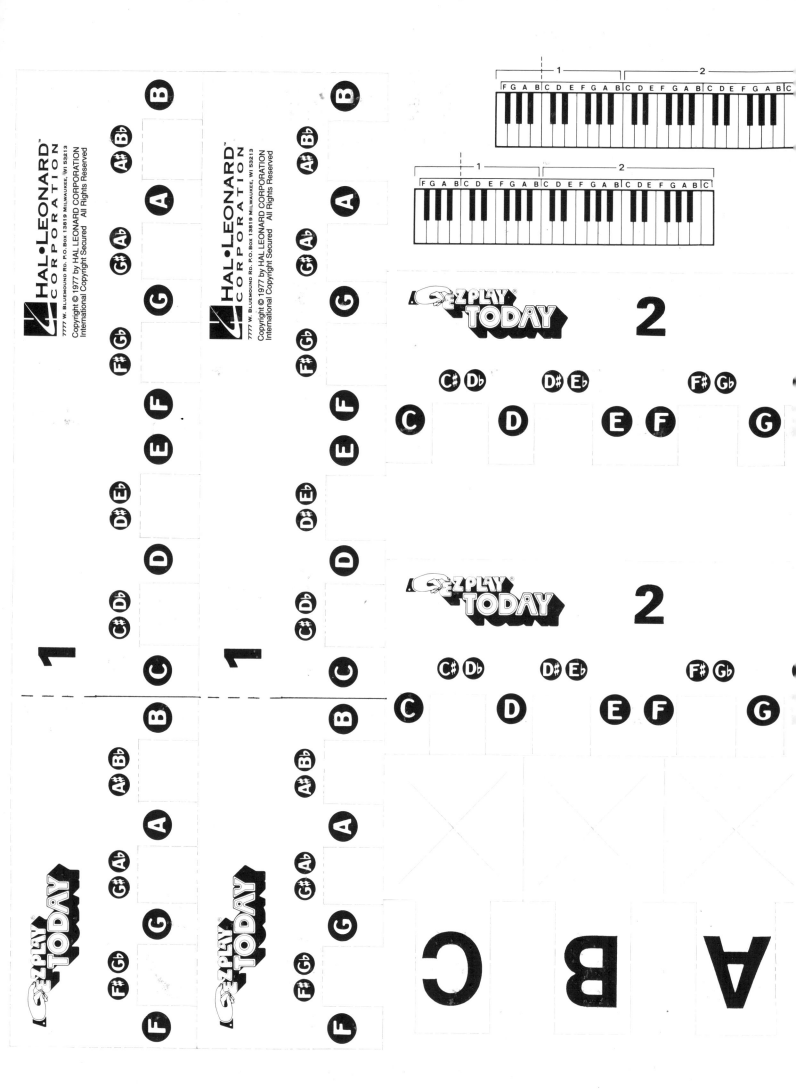

Punch out guides and slide over the pro- per pedals in this manner:

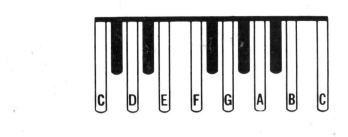

(Console Organs: Cut off letter name por- tion of tabs and attach to the proper pedals with clear tape.)

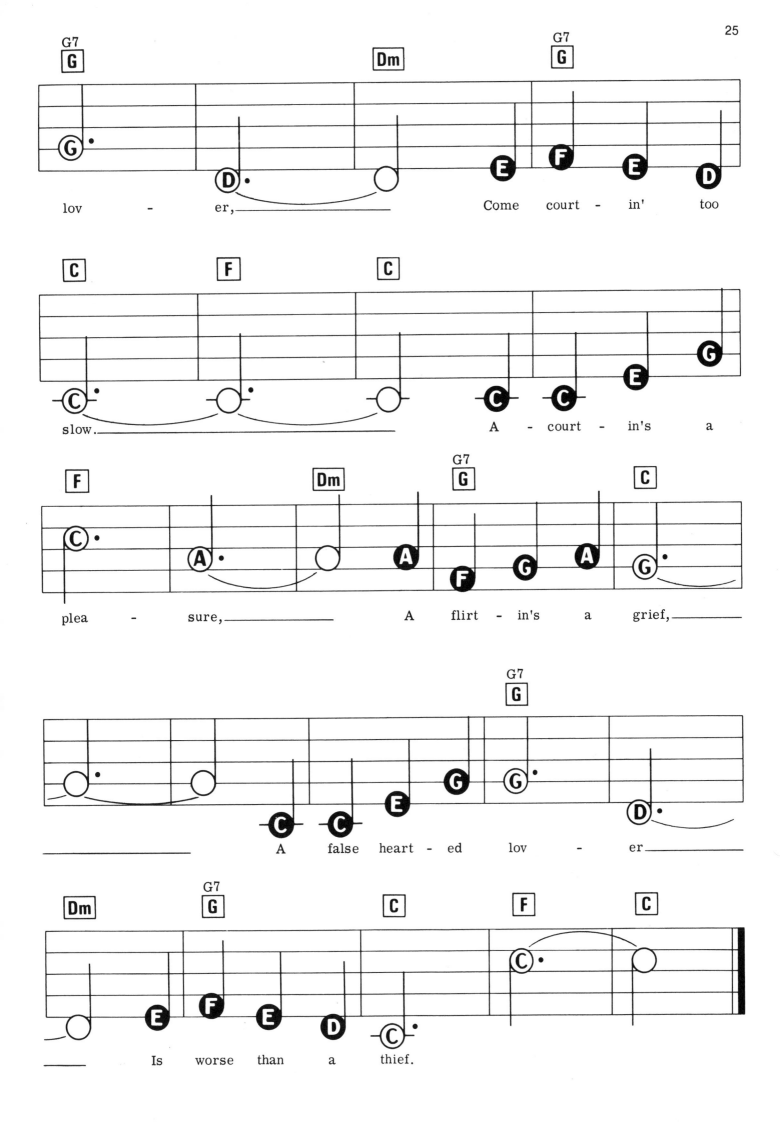

INTRODUCING - EIGHTH NOTES

● A single eighth note has a flag on its stem, and it receives 1/2 beat.

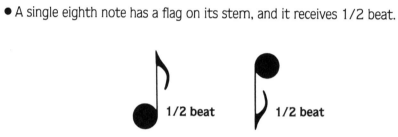

● Two or more eighth notes are written in a group and connected by a beam.

Two eighth notes equal one full beat

2 beats

● To play and correctly count eighth notes, divide your counting of each beat into two parts by saying "and" between the numbered beats.

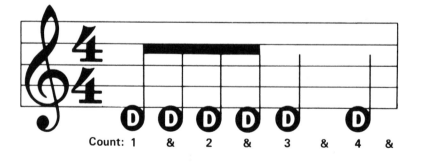

Count: 1   &   2   &   3   &   4   &

Lavender's Blue

Registration 2
Rhythm: Waltz

English

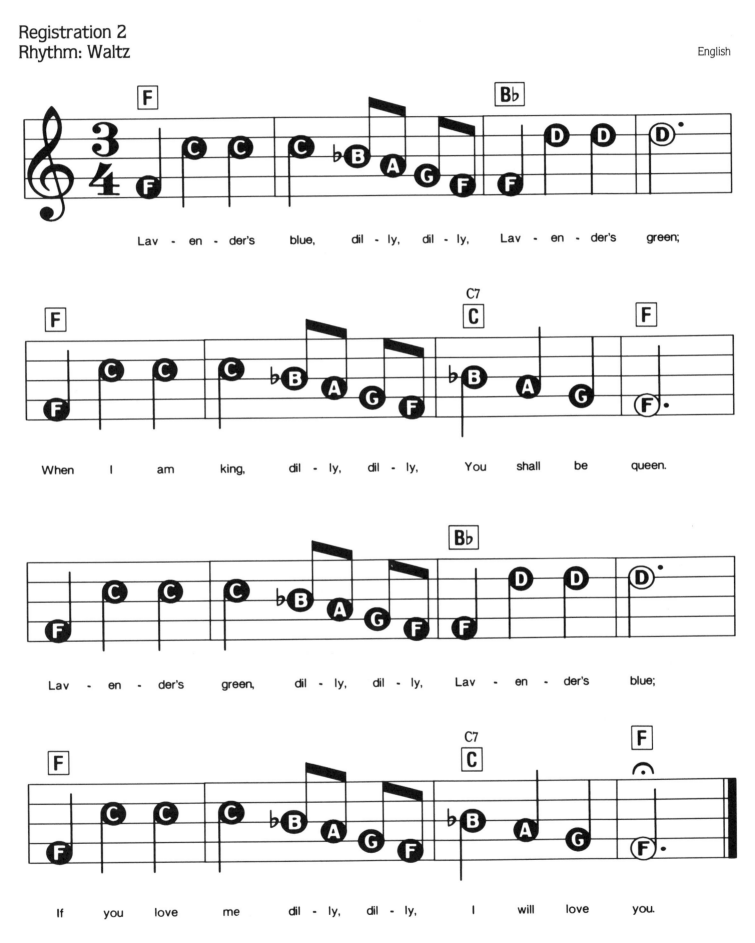

Lav - en - der's blue, dil - ly, dil - ly, Lav - en - der's green;

When I am king, dil - ly, dil - ly, You shall be queen.

Lav - en - der's green, dil - ly, dil - ly, Lav - en - der's blue;

If you love me dil - ly, dil - ly, I will love you.

INTRODUCING - THE DOTTED QUARTER NOTE

- A dot placed after any note increases the length of that note by one half.

- As previously illustrated, the dotted half note receives three beats.

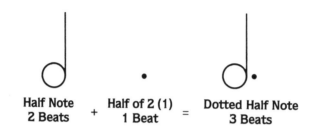

Half Note   Half of 2 (1)   Dotted Half Note
2 Beats   +   1 Beat   =   3 Beats

- The same principle applies to the dotted quarter note.

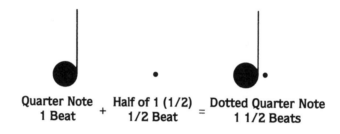

Quarter Note   Half of 1 (1/2)   Dotted Quarter Note
1 Beat   +   1/2 Beat   =   1 1/2 Beats

- The dotted quarter note is usually followed by an eighth note.

1 1/2 Beats   1/2 Beat

- Study and play this counting example.

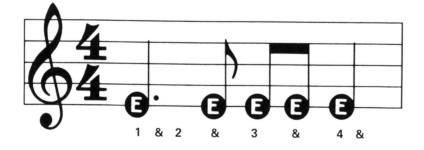

INTRODUCING - A NEW CHORD: D

- ● ONE KEY or CHORD BUTTON — Locate the key or button labeled D. If your automatic chord unit does not have the D chord, play the alternate chord D7.

- ● STANDARD CHORD — D = F♯ A D

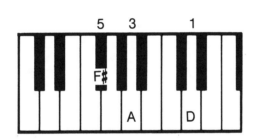

She Wore A Yellow Ribbon

Registration 4
Rhythm: Swing or March

Traditional

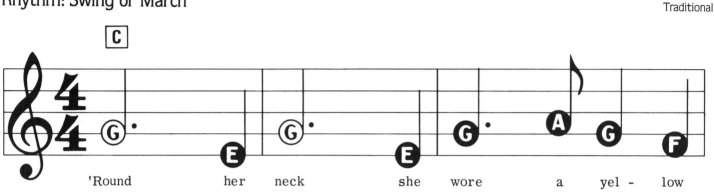

'Round her neck she wore a yel - low

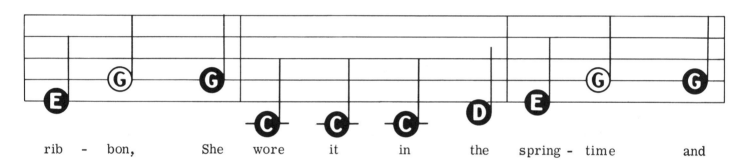

rib - bon, She wore it in the spring - time and

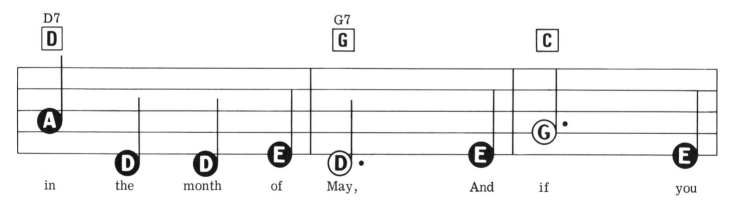

in the month of May, And if you

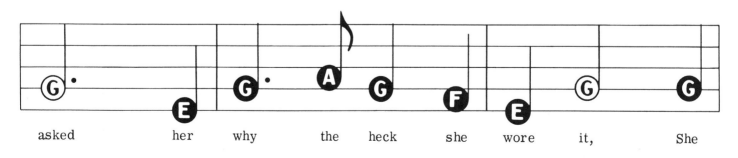

asked her why the heck she wore it, She

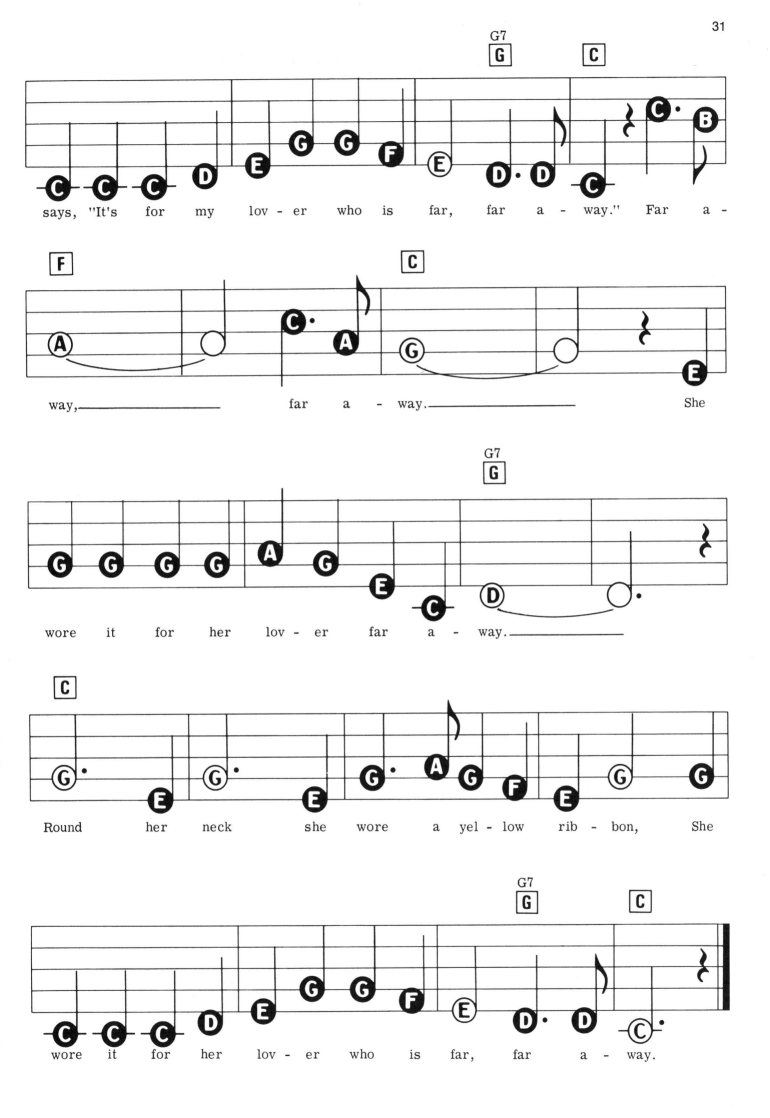

INTRODUCING - A NEW NOTE

To be able to play your next song, you'll need to learn the staff and keyboard location of another "G."

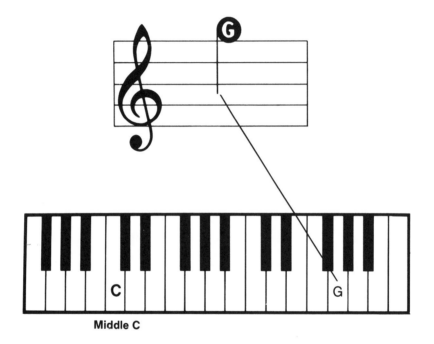

Middle C

INTRODUCING - THE SHARP SIGN (♯)

When a sharp sign appears to the left of any note, raise the note one half step.
In other words, play the first adjacent key to the right.

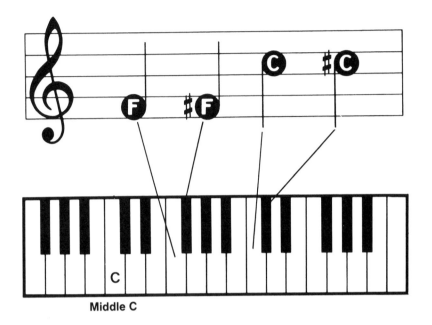

INTRODUCING - D.S. al CODA

This is another type of repeat sign. The letters D.S. mean "from the sign." The entire term means to:

• Return to the sign 𝄋 .

• Repeat to this sign: ⊕.

• Skip to the section marked CODA and play to the end.

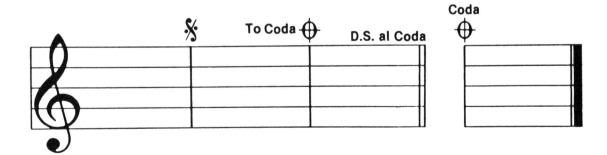

Londonderry Air

Registration 1
Rhythm: Ballad or Rock

Irish

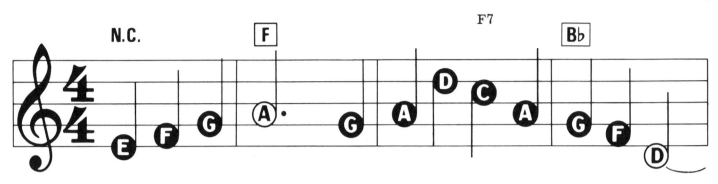

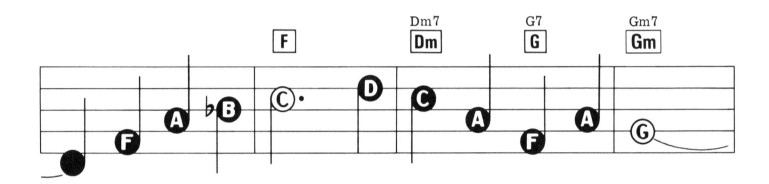

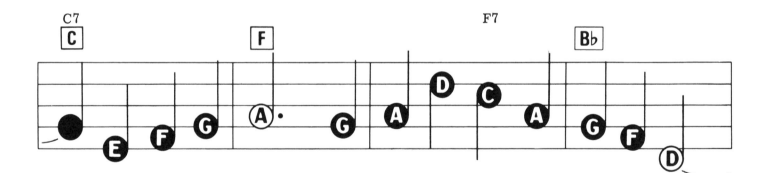

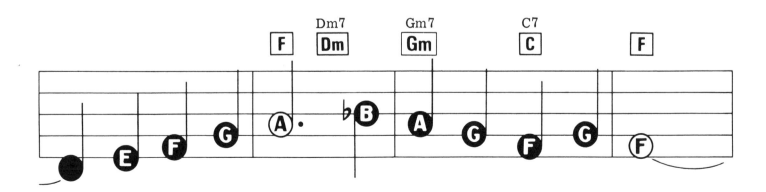

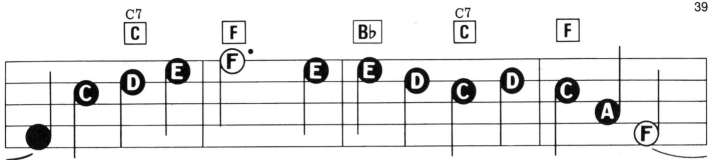

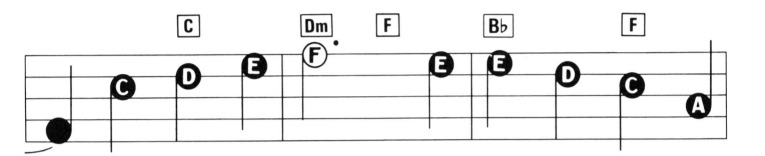

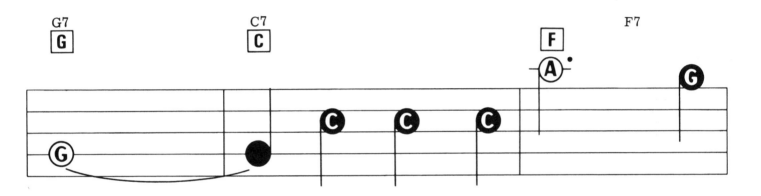

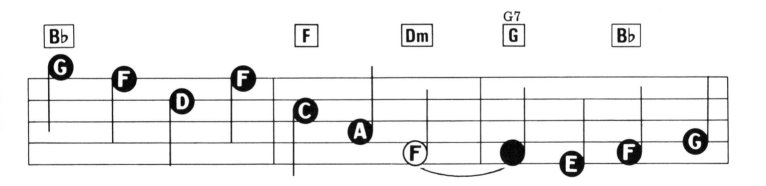

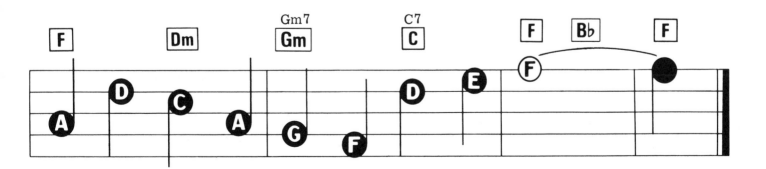

I Gave My Love A Cherry

Registration 2
Rhythm: Slow Rock

Traditional

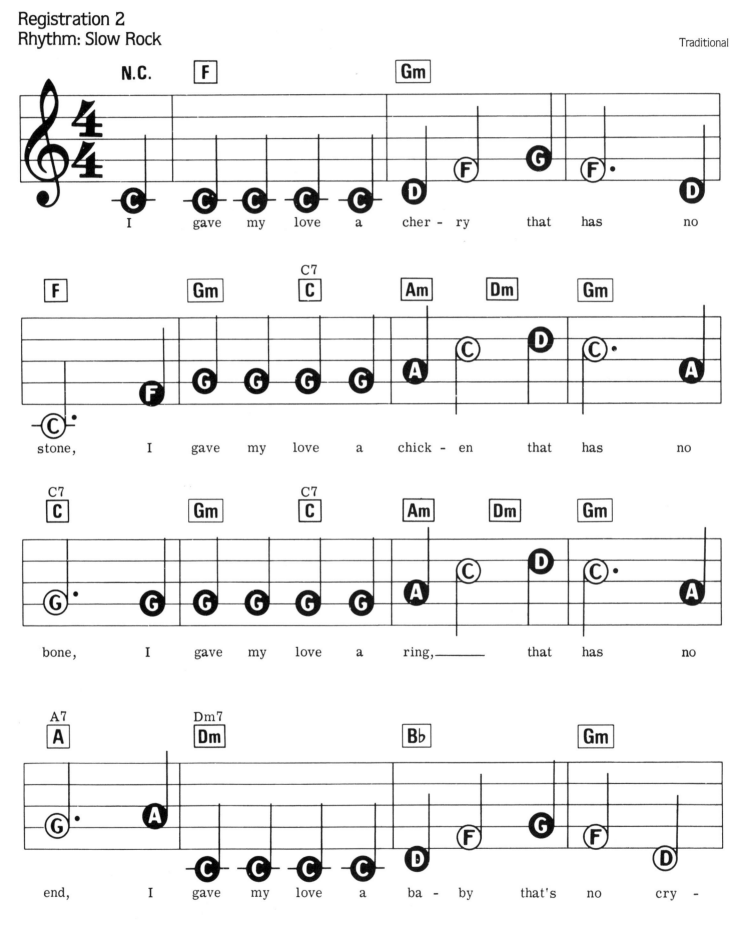

41

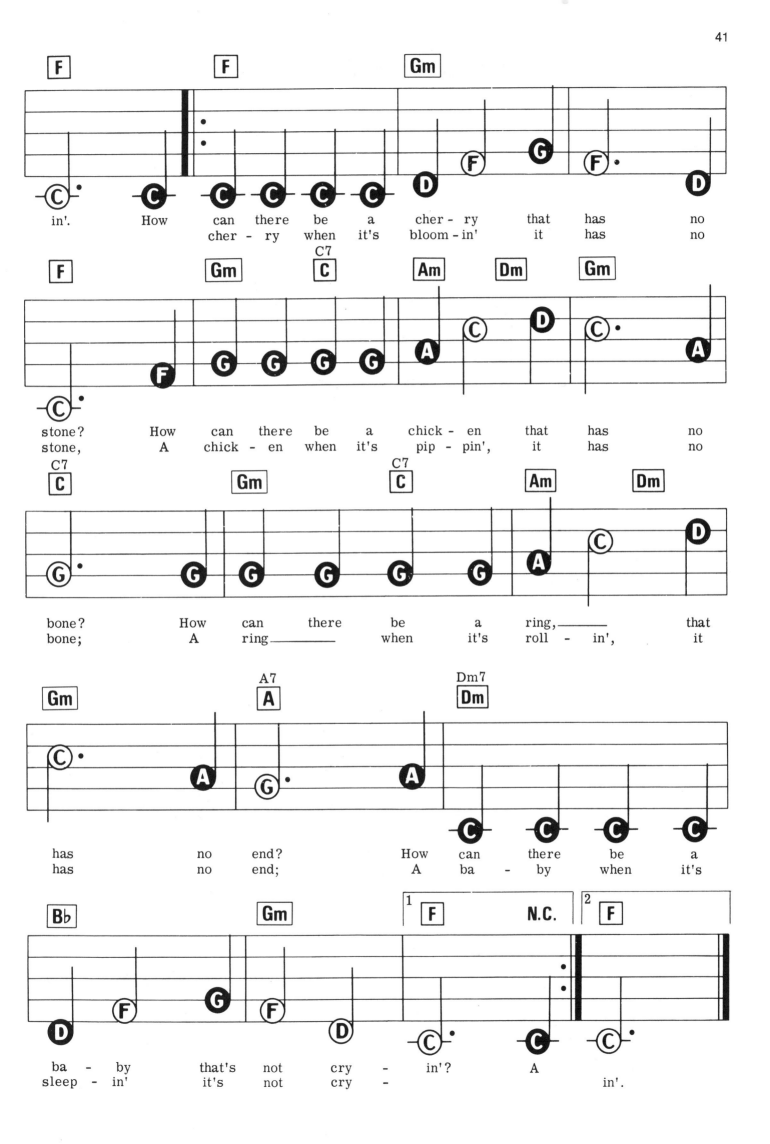

44

NOTATION AND TERMS

For your reference, the following is a review of music notation and terms introduced in BEGINNINGS Book A.

E-Z Play® TODAY Notes

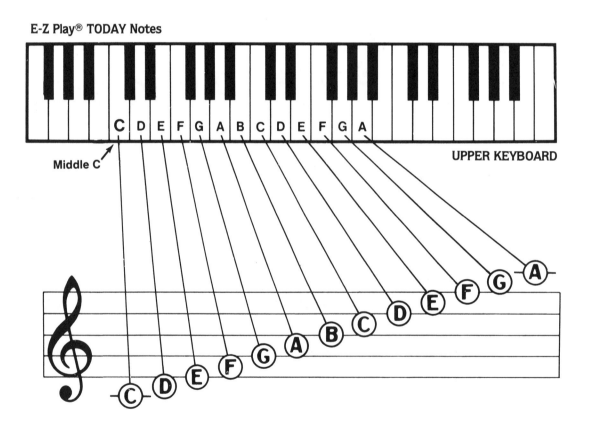

Note Values

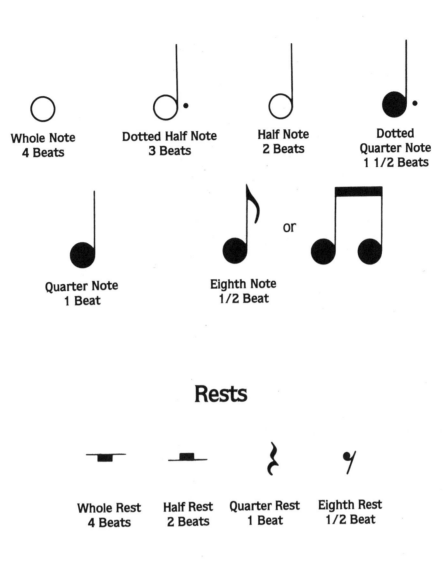

Whole Note
4 Beats

Dotted Half Note
3 Beats

Half Note
2 Beats

Dotted Quarter Note
1 1/2 Beats

Quarter Note
1 Beat

Eighth Note
1/2 Beat

or

Rests

Whole Rest
4 Beats

Half Rest
2 Beats

Quarter Rest
1 Beat

Eighth Rest
1/2 Beat

Repeat Signs

D.S. al Coda — Return to 𝄋 , play up to "To Coda," skip to "Coda" section.

Repeat and Fade — Repeat to beginning or to last repeat sign, and gradually fade out by decreasing the volume.

Chords

●CHORDS (ONE KEY or CHORD BUTTON)

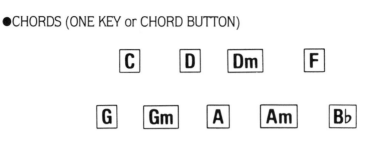

● STANDARD CHORD POSITIONS—Refer to the Chord Speller Chart on the next page for playing chords used in the E-Z Play TODAY music arrangements.

Chord Symbols With Arrows

In some books in the E-Z Play TODAY Music Series, you may find chord symbols that have one or more arrows inside the chord box. These refer to chords that include one or more black keys. An arrow to the left of the chord name indicates a flat; an arrow to the right of the chord name indicates a sharp.

N.C.

This is an abbreviation for No Chord. Do not play a chord or pedal until the next chord symbol appears.

Chord Speller Chart
of Standard Chord Positions

For those who play standard chord positions, all chords used in the E-Z Play TODAY music arrangements are shown here in their most commonly used chord positions. Suggested fingering is also indicated, but feel free to use alternate fingering.

CHORD FAMILY Abbrev.	MAJOR	MINOR (m)	7TH (7)	MINOR 7TH (m7)
C	5 2 1 G-C-E	5 2 1 G-C-Eb	5 3 2 1 G-Bb-C-E	5 3 2 1 G-Bb-C-Eb
Db	5 2 1 Ab-Db-F	5 2 1 Ab-Db-E	5 3 2 1 Ab-B-Db-F	5 3 2 1 Ab-B-Db-E
D	5 3 1 F#-A-D	5 2 1 A-D-F	5 3 2 1 F#-A-C-D	5 3 2 1 A-C-D-F
Eb	5 3 1 G-Bb-Eb	5 3 1 Gb-Bb-Eb	5 3 2 1 G-Bb-Db-Eb	5 3 2 1 Gb-Bb-Db-Eb
E	5 3 1 G#-B-E	5 3 1 G-B-E	5 3 2 1 G#-B-D-E	5 3 2 1 G-B-D-E
F	4 2 1 A-C-F	4 2 1 Ab-C-F	5 3 2 1 A-C-Eb-F	5 3 2 1 Ab-C-Eb-F
F#	4 2 1 F#-A#-C#	4 2 1 F#-A-C#	5 3 2 1 F#-A#-C#-E	5 3 2 1 F#-A-C#-E
G	5 3 1 G-B-D	5 3 1 G-Bb-D	5 3 2 1 G-B-D-F	5 3 2 1 G-Bb-D-F
Ab	4 2 1 Ab-C-Eb	4 2 1 Ab-B-Eb	5 3 2 1 Ab-C-Eb-Gb	5 3 2 1 Ab-B-Eb-Gb
A	4 2 1 A-C#-E	4 2 1 A-C-E	5 4 2 1 G-A-C#-E	5 4 2 1 G-A-C-E
Bb	4 2 1 Bb-D-F	4 2 1 Bb-Db-F	5 4 2 1 Ab-Bb-D-F	5 4 2 1 Ab-Bb-Db-F
B	5 2 1 F#-B-D#	5 2 1 F#-B-D	5 3 2 1 F#-A-B-D#	5 3 2 1 F#-A-B-D

Registration Guide

- Match the Registration number on the song to the corresponding numbered category below. Select and activate an instrumental sound available on your instrument.

- Choose an automatic rhythm appropriate to the mood and style of the song. (Consult your Owner's Guide for proper operation of automatic rhythm features.)

- Adjust the tempo and volume controls to comfortable settings.

Registration

1	Flutes, Clarinet, Oboe, Flugel Horn, Trombone, French Horn, Organ Flutes
2	Saxophones, Trumpet, Mute Trumpet, Synth Leads, Jazz/Gospel Organs
3	Acoustic/Electric Guitars, Banjo, Mandolin, Dulcimer, Ukulele, Hawaiian Guitar
4	Violin, Viola, Cello, Fiddle, String Ensemble, Pizzicato, Organ Strings
5	Vibraphone, Marimba, Xylophone, Steel Drums, Bells, Celesta, Chimes
6	Accordion, French Accordion, Mussette, Harmonica, Pump Organ, Bagpipes
7	Pipe Organ, Hand Bells, Vocal Ensemble, Choir, Organ Flutes
8	Piano, Electric Piano, Honky Tonk Piano, Harpsichord, Clavi
9	Melodic Percussion, Wah Trumpet, Synth, Whistle, Kazoo, Perc. Organ
10	Bass Section, Sax Section, Wind Ensemble, Full Organ, Theater Organ